AN AUTISM DIAGNOSIS MUST COME FROM A LICENSED PROFESSIONAL

OUR MISSION:

SHARE THAT EVERY CHILD ON THE AUTISM SPECTRUM IS UNIQUE, BUT NOT ALONE.

PROVIDE A CREATIVE OUTLET FOR AUTISTIC CHILDREN TO LEARN ABOUT THEMSELVES.

SPREAD AUTISM AWARENESS THROUGH RELATABLE REAL LIFE SCENARIOS TO FOSTER STRONGER RELATIONSHIPS IN THEIR COMMUNITY.

"Jelly Bean Needs Routine" Text and Illustrations © 2024
ALL RIGHTS RESERVED BY JEI PRODUCTIONS LLC

FIRST EDITION, 2024

This book is not intended as a substitute for medical advice. The reader should consult a licensed professional in matters relating to their health, particularly with respect to any symptoms that may require diagnosis or medical attention.

No part of this book may be used or reproduced in any manner whatsoever without written permission except in the case of brief quotations embodied in clerical articles and reviews.

All characters appearing in this work are fictitious. Any resemblance to real persons, living or dead, is purely coincidental.

Publisher's Cataloging-in-Publication
(Provided by Cassidy Cataloguing Services, Inc.)

Names: Renee, Missi, author. | Paj, Eduardo, illustrator.

Title: Jelly Bean needs routine / written by Missi Renee ; illustrated by Eduardo Paj.

Description: First edition. | [Arvada, Colorado] : JEI Productions LLC, [2024] | Series: Kids spectrum stories. | Audience: Elementary school children. Summary: Change in day-to-day routine can be really hard, especially for children on the Autism Spectrum. In this book, Jelly Bean and her dad discover the usefulness of a schedule and Jelly Bean shows how to use tools to calm down when she's upset.--Publisher.

Identifiers: ISBN: 979-8-9899915-2-5 (Paperback) | 979-8-9899915-3-2 (Hardcover) | LCCN: 2024905947

Subjects: LCSH: Autism in children--Juvenile literature. | Autism spectrum disorders in children-- Juvenile lit-erature. | Scheduling--Psychological aspects--Juvenile literature. | Stress management for children--Juvenile lit-erature. | Anxiety in children--Treatment--Juvenile literature. | Calmness--Juvenile literature. | CYAC: Autism. | Stress management. | Anxiety. | Calmness. | LCGFT: Picture books. | BISAC: FAMILY & RELATIONSHIPS / Autism Spectrum Disorders. | FAMILY & RELATIONSHIPS / Children with Special Needs. | PSYCHOLOGY / Psychopathology / Autism Spectrum Disorders.

Classification: LCC: RJ506.A9 M37 2024 | DDC: 616.85/882--dc23

Learn more about us at
www.kidsspectrumstories.com

JELLY BEAN
Needs Routine

Written by Missi Renee
Illustrated by Eduardo Paj

This is Jelly Bean.

She likes to go to the same places and stay in her routine.

When things change,
Jelly Bean doesn't know what to expect.

This can make her feel nervous or upset.

Jelly Bean has a schedule by her bed telling her what will happen each day.

She woke up Saturday morning, looked at her schedule and said, "Yes! It's library day! I need more books!"

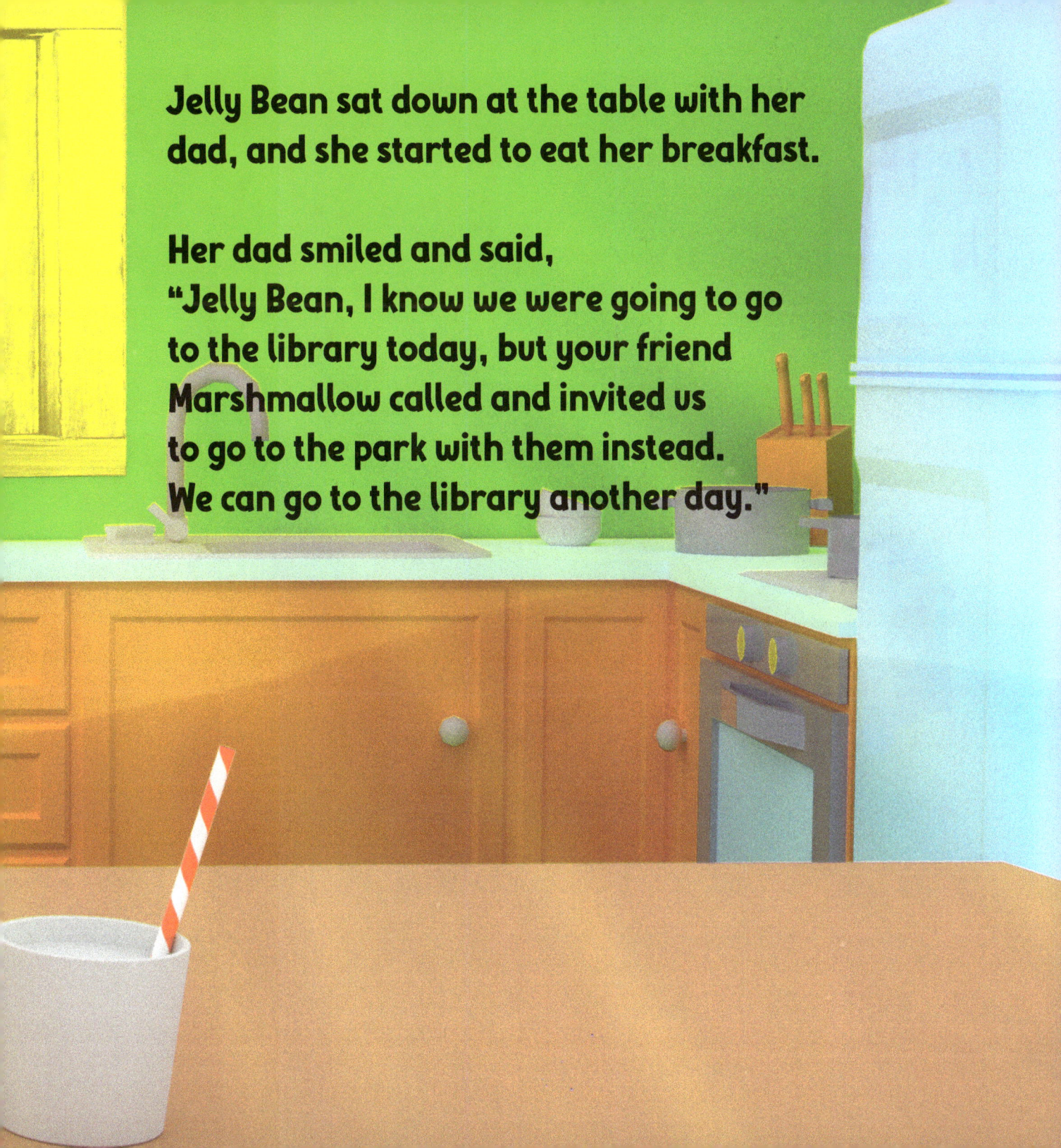

Jelly Bean sat down at the table with her dad, and she started to eat her breakfast.

Her dad smiled and said, "Jelly Bean, I know we were going to go to the library today, but your friend Marshmallow called and invited us to go to the park with them instead. We can go to the library another day."

This change made Jelly Bean feel anxious and frustrated.

She yelled back, "Why? We go to the library on Saturdays!" and she ran to her room.

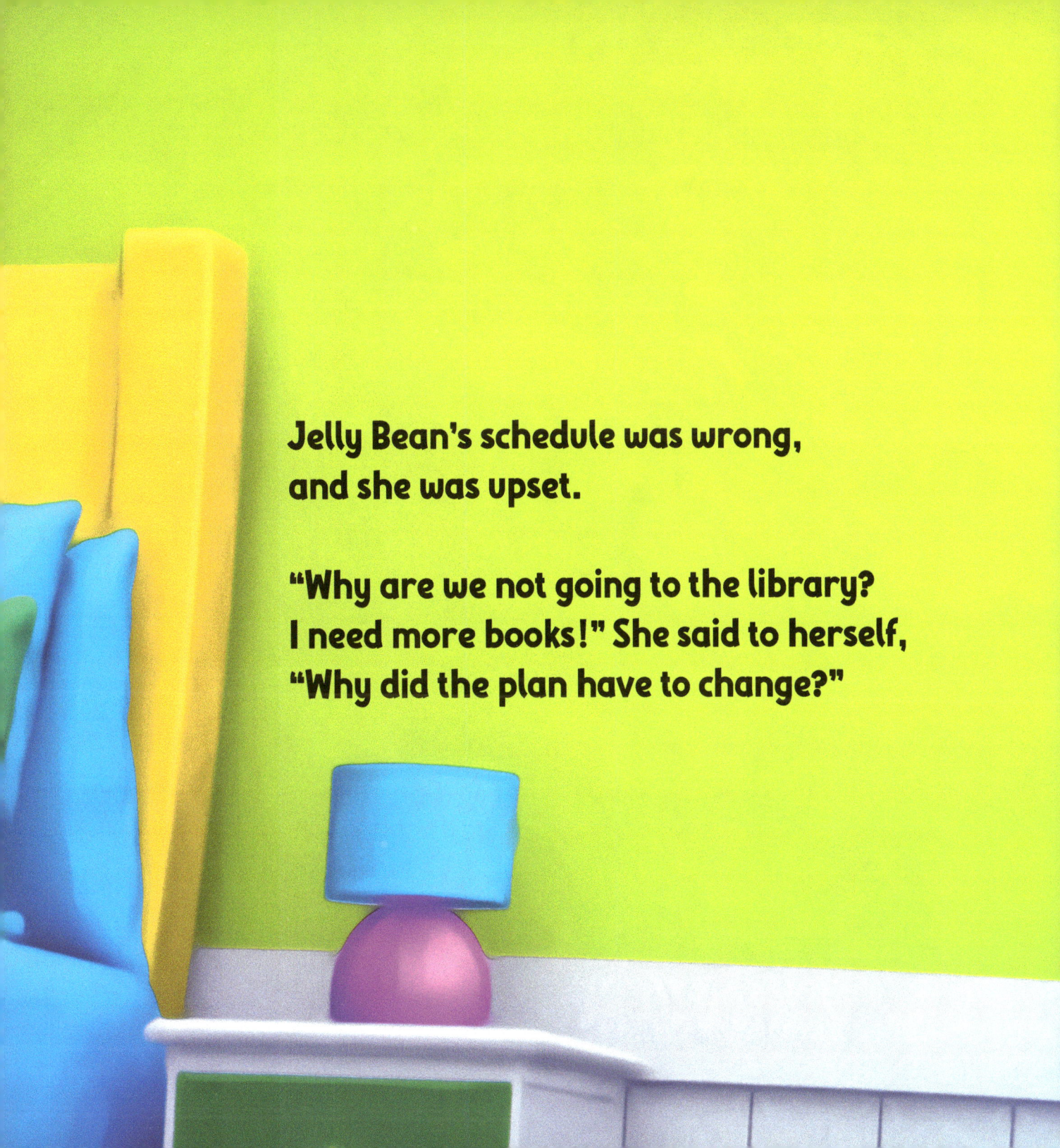

Jelly Bean's schedule was wrong, and she was upset.

"Why are we not going to the library? I need more books!" She said to herself, "Why did the plan have to change?"

Jelly Bean took some deep breaths and cuddled her favorite stuffed owl.

Cuddling her stuffed owl helps Jelly Bean calm her body down when she has big feelings.

Jelly Bean's dad was confused
and frustrated by her reaction.

He thought Jelly Bean would want to see her friend.

Then her dad stopped to think about what happened.

He knew that making changes, even to do something fun, could be hard for Jelly Bean.

Jelly Bean's dad walked into her room and said, "I am sorry, Jelly Bean. I know change is hard for you."

"Next time we change our plan, we will sit down and talk about it. That way we can make the new plan together and put it on your schedule."

Jelly Bean liked this idea.

She still doesn't like when things change, but knowing about the change sooner and seeing it on her schedule really helps.

Jelly Bean's dad called Marshmallow's family and made plans to join them at the park another day.

Jelly Bean saw her dad write "Park with Marshmallow" on the schedule by her bed, and they went to the library.

www.ingramcontent.com/pod-product-compliance
Lightning Source LLC
Chambersburg PA
CBHW061402010526
44119CB00010B/236